TIMELESS TREASURES

OTHER RAND EDITIONS/TOFUA PRESS PUBLICATIONS

San Diego County Place Names, by Lou Stein

We Three Came West: A True Chronicle; Helen Raitt and
Mary Collier Wayne, Editors

Scripps Institution of Oceanography: Probing the Oceans
1936 to 1976, by Elizabeth N. Shor

TIMELESS TREASURES
SAN DIEGO'S
VICTORIAN HERITAGE

Photographs by Karen Johl

Text by Karen Johl with Jane Lowrie Miller

Rand Editions
San Diego

Cover photo: The Long-Waterman House

Copyright © 1982 by Karen A. Johl
First Edition
Published by Rand Editions
10457-F Roselle Street
San Diego, California 92121

Editor: Elizabeth Rand
Cover and Design: David Scott

Library of Congress Catalog Card Number 81-86088
ISBN 0-914488-26-0

The excerpt from *A Gift to the Street* on page ix is reprinted with permission of the author, Carol Olwell. Antelope Island Press, 1976.

Dedication

In loving memory of my photography teacher and friend, Mac Miller

Contents

Preface

When Victorian houses were a common sight in San Diego, we did not give a great deal of thought to our loss each time one was torn down. As they became fewer in number, we began to realize that perhaps they were worth saving, for when they are gone, we will never be able to view their splendor again.

San Diego has a Victorian architectural heritage that, while not as remarkable as San Francisco's, is splendid nonetheless. A number of fine examples remain, many of which were built during San Diego's "boom" period in the late 1880s. These old houses are concentrated in several areas, corresponding to the early growth patterns of San Diego. As the population increased and public and private transportation became more available, neighborhoods reached farther and farther out.

Most of the Victorian houses were built before the turn of the century. During the early 1900s, Victorian-style architecture with its gingerbread and frills generally fell into disfavor.

Shortly after I moved to San Diego about six years ago, I decided to document the surviving examples of San Diego's Victorian heritage. I quickly realized that there are many more Victorian houses remaining than I had first imagined. When I would find one of these houses I felt as if I had discovered a treasure, a rose in bloom hidden in a patch of weeds.

As I set out to study and photograph these treasures, I found, in many cases, peeling paint and sagging porches. Then I began to meet dozens of people who are in some way contributing to the preservation of our heritage. Paint buckets, scaffolding, the sound of hammers, and tired, paint-spattered people greeted me during my travels through San Diego's historic neighborhoods.

Many of the city's showplace homes where lavish parties were once held are now living second lives as office buildings, restaurants, shops, and even a charming photography studio. The interiors of most of the homes and businesses are not open for public tours, but I recommend that you go on neighborhood walking tours to discover these survivors of an age gone by.

While I was not able to include every one of the houses, I hope that this book can be a fitting tribute to all of the Victorians and to the people who care so much for them. The people were a joy to meet, and their houses are truly a joy to behold.

Karen Johl
San Diego, California

"But why am I so fond of these buildings? Because such houses as these will never be built on earth again . . ."

Carol Olwell
A Gift to the Street
Antelope Island Press, 1976

A Special Thank You...

...to Elizabeth Rand of Rand Editions, my publisher and friend, for her constant help and encouragement over the past three years. For her expert editing of the text, and for letting me know that she had faith in this project through all of its ups and downs, my grateful thanks.

...to Patricia Schaelchlin, my friend and expert advisor in matters historical, for her help and suggestions, and for never being too busy to give generously and cheerfully of her time and knowledge.

...to Jane Lowrie Miller, my friend and literary consultant, for her competent assistance with the text of this book and for her encouragement when I needed it most.

...to Sylvia Arden, Head Librarian/Archivist at San Diego Historical Society Library and Manuscripts Collection, for her professionalism and her instinctive ability to suggest research sources I would not otherwise have seen.

...to David Scott for his beautiful design of this book and for being a most generous, friendly, and competent person to work with.

...to Patricia Schmitt and Jeff Johnson of Rand Editions for their kindness and enthusiasm.

...to Carol Olwell, co-author of *A Gift to the Street*, for her beautiful book which was my first inspiration, and for her kind correspondence that helped many times to buoy my spirits.

...and to the following individuals and groups for their encouragement and support: Bill Ballance, Larry and Jane Booth, Rick Crawford, John and Mary Lee Deckard, Rhoda Kruse, Carl Lock, Alexandra Luberski, Tom Scharf, Joan Zeenkov, my family, the SOHO volunteers, the Mac Miller Photography Club, the San Diego Historical Society, and my fellow respiratory therapists.

Introduction

by Patricia Schaelchlin

How many early Victorian houses are left in San Diego, and are they worth the effort needed to save them? *Timeless Treasures*, an album of these houses, answers these questions in an objective way — and in so doing makes an important contribution to the city.

From this pictorial collection, it is apparent that many Victorian houses — more than we thought — still stand today. There may well be hundreds of these houses, for they cluster in neighborhoods on streets where we don't often travel. They are old and they look it — with paint rubbed off and redwood siding bare, with broken windows and weed-strewn yards — but still recognizable, for you can't deny the distinctive Victorian architecture. But maybe more importantly, *Timeless Treasures*, with its honest photographs, reveals a sense of place, a recognition of where we *are* and where we *were*.

It is this sense of place that encourages preservation. As a link with the architectural past, it transports us back in time a hundred or more years, imposing a uniqueness that is transmitted generation after generation, not lost as long as the houses stand. Families live in these houses, and whether they recognize it or not, they are aware of this sense of place. It is here that they live; it is here and now that contact must be made, before demolition is a threat. It is here that advocacy preservation can begin.

Preservationists, used to crisis situations, can now meet with owners in a constructive way. The past two decades have witnessed a confrontation between those who wish to save and those who wished to develop. Many buildings have been preserved; the Santa Fe Depot, the Villa Montezuma, Horton Plaza, the Long-Waterman House, the Heritage Park buildings, and the San Diego Rowing Club boathouse were all to be demolished, and only through the preservation efforts do they remain. Because of these successes, and in this time of concern for cost-effectiveness, the owners of vintage properties are beginning to see them as assets. They are rehabilitating the properties and realizing profitable returns by renting them as offices, deluxe apartments, and even bed and board hotels. Victorian houses are again becoming a valuable commodity.

With this new interest in restoration, the preservationists must reevaluate their goals and their role. For the first time, there is an opportunity to implement advocacy preservation. Some of the small neighborhood communities have so far been ignored by urban renewal, but given their prime central core location, they may well — and soon — be endangered by large development. Their future can be directed to preservation if revitalization is begun now.

And it is here that it can begin. By encouraging the owners to get together with neighbors and plan for their community future, by painting the homes, cleaning up the yards and facing the environmental problems, owners can turn these areas into prime properties, raising their value and bringing a cohesiveness and new vitality to the neighborhoods. The preservationist's role is to bring about the awareness that there is a choice, to help in finding financial support, to assist in organization and to show that it is profitable both in money and in satisfaction.

Timeless Treasures identifies for us our city's treasures: some of them mansions, many of them the small houses where most of the early San Diegans lived. After an era of protecting the grand architecture of the city, it is time to turn our attention to the less ornate, those pattern-book neighborhood houses that were built in the thousands — and it is only because of their quantity that we still see them today.

Timeless Treasures is further important, and will become increasingly so, because it contains many houses that have never been photographed so well. Some of theses houses will be lost, and nowhere else will there be evidence that they were ever here. They have been recorded as timeless city treasures and may well be saved because of it.

THE HEART OF
NEW SAN DIEGO

Downtown 1867

Looking over the city today, it is hard to imagine downtown San Diego (south of Date Street) as it was in the early days. Horses, wagons, and carriages plied the downtown streets, raising clouds of dust in their wake. Shops, banks, hotels, livery stables, blacksmiths, and other businesses and trades of the day lined Fifth Avenue.

Steamships making the run from San Francisco deposited passengers at the Fifth Avenue wharf, built in 1869 by Alonzo E. Horton. Shortly after his arrival in San Diego in 1867, Horton had bought for $265.00 a parcel of land comprising 960 acres (Horton's Addition), part of which is now downtown. This area gradually replaced Old Town as the city's hub.

When Horton purchased the addition, cattle and sheep grazed on the sagebrush-covered land. By 1870, ungraded and treeless streets had been laid out and small, crude buildings erected. Since the wharf was located at its foot, Fifth Avenue emerged as the main street of the new city.

Mr. Horton built his first house at 10th and G Streets, a gabled home with a fireplace in every room. (Unfortunately, neither this nor Horton's later homes is standing today.)

During the boom of the '80s, many houses were built in San Diego as the population increased from approximately 2,500 to 40,000. The downtown area grew rapidly with the construction of a number of large business buildings, many of which remain today. The houses that were built during this time were of the "gingerbread" variety. No matter how simple, each one had some sort of ornamentation, even if only some decorative brackets under the eaves or some fishscale shingles.

During the decades of the 1950s and '60s, parts of the downtown area gradually fell into decay as the developing suburbs, with their shopping centers, office buildings, and industrial parks, drew business from downtown. In 1969 the first glimmerings of hope for downtown rehabilitation came with the concept of a rebirth of the Gaslamp District.

The remaining Victorian houses in the downtown area are largely serving as rooming houses and office buildings. Several are faced with the possible threat of demolition to make way for parking lots. The houses in Victoria Square in the heart of downtown are a testament to how effectively the old can coexist with the new.

1502 6th Avenue

A corner entrance and parapet are among the features of this richly decorated office building, built in 1895 as a residence.

1543 7th Avenue

A beautiful Queen Anne tower house survives on a block where other Victorians have been torn down. It now serves as a boarding house.

4

This photograph shows the proximity to downtown.

One of the few remaining granite markers to be found at a San Diego house.

1407 2nd Avenue THE KIESSIG HOUSE, 1894

Historical Site #110

The Kiessig House was built in 1894. The original owner, Charles Kiessig, came to San Diego in 1886 and was active in San Diego real estate. He owned a gun shop until his death in 1914. The house was owned and occupied by the Kiessig family for 82 years. In 1976 an attorney purchased and named Victoria Square and restored the three houses located there. The Kiessig House has been virtually unchanged since its construction. It now is a popular downtown pub.

230 Cedar Street

Simplicity of style with straight clean lines distinguishes this Italianate Victorian from its more ornate counterparts.

1658 Front Street

Another Italianate (ca. 1888), a bit more ornate, features decorative brackets and a unique sawtooth front porch design. The arched windows, not often found in San Diego Victorians, lend a graceful touch.

734 10th Avenue

This Italianate Victorian (late 1870s) close to downtown is now an apartment house.

1600 Block of Union Street

Perhaps the only complete block
of Victorian houses in the city.

1632 Union Street

Historical Site #123

This Queen Anne residence (ca. 1880-1886) is decorated with a large sunburst design and various shingle designs.

1610 Union Street

Almost identical in style to its neighbor, another Queen Anne is currently used as an apartment house. Though similar, they had different builders.

12

1610 Union Street
The sunburst-adorned gable is nearly identical in the two
neighboring houses.

A side view (south) of 1610 Union Street.

1665 Union Street

This house, now an insurance office, features beautiful bracket and spindle work and a dentil course under the eaves.

1620 Union Street

The morning sun casts lacy shadows on this small (ca. 1888) decorative cottage, now serving as an office building.

205 West Date Street THE SILBERHORN HOUSE

This Italianate Victorian (ca. 1895) has had no apparent alterations. In 1922 it was the home of George Karl Silberhorn, a Spanish War veteran.

16

SAN DIEGO
SPREADS EASTWARD

Sherman Heights 1870s

In June 1867 Matthew Sherman bought a 160-acre parcel of land from the City of San Diego, for 50 cents an acre. Sherman's eighty-dollar investment provided satisfactory grazing land for his herd of sheep until he subdivided his parcel and named it Sherman's Addition. (This was shortly after Alonzo Horton bought his addition in 1867 in the heart of what is now downtown.)

Sherman's Addition is bounded by 14th, 24th, Market and Commercial Streets. Sherman built his first house on 19th near J Street, where it stands today. He donated land for a school on the site of the present-day Sherman School.

Sometime after 1885, Sherman built a large home at 22nd and Market, at a cost of $15,000. The house is still there, though altered so radically that little of its Victorian charm remains.

The development of Sherman Heights, as this area came to be called, closely followed that of Golden Hill, its neighbor directly to the north. Highway 94 now separates the two communities and has somewhat altered the boundaries of Sherman Heights.

The jewel of Sherman Heights is the lavishly constructed Villa Montezuma, once a curiosity of early San Diego, now a museum for all to enjoy. In the early days, many social events were held there; now neighbors and tourists alike may explore this eclectic Victorian home (operated by the San Diego Historical Society) or attend the cultural events that are held at the Villa.

2412 J Street THE LIVINGSTON HOUSE

Historical Site # 58

The Livingston House was built in 1887 for a Mrs. C. Morris Livingston at a cost of $5,000. The house, built largely of redwood, contains 13 rooms and 52 windows. From 1933-1969 it was a boarding house and was saved from demolition in 1970.

542 21st Street

Almost identical gables and porch railings adorn the next three houses, located only a few blocks apart.

171 21st Street

2419 J Street

This picturesque Queen Anne Victorian is accented by a white picket fence and iron cresting around the balcony. The house has been divided into apartments since 1936. The design was probably originally the same as the preceding two houses.

22

2260 Island Avenue

Squared bay windows and a portico accent this apartment house. The roof was possibly adorned with iron cresting at one time. Most of the iron ornamentation on Victorian houses was removed either because it made the roof leak, for wartime scrap metal drives, or to modernize the house.

1925 K Street

THE VILLA MONTEZUMA, 1887

Historical Site #11
Historic American Buildings Survey #432
National Register of Historic Places

The Villa Montezuma is probably San Diego's most unusual Victorian house, both architecturally and historically. The house, with its towers, gargoyles, and jewel-like stained glass windows, seems to loom an anachronism in its Sherman Heights neighborhood. Built in 1887 by San Diego citizens for Benjamin Jesse Francis Shepard, a world-renowned concert pianist and later an author and essayist, the house was designed to his specifications by architects Comstock and Trotsche.

The design of the house reflects Shepard's love of art, literature, and music. Born in 1848 in Birkenhead, England, Shepard spent his early years in Illinois — years he wrote about in a novel, *Valley of the Shadows,* written under his pen name of Francis Grierson. At the age of 21 he began to travel and found his way into the salons of Paris. He performed in concert before the crowned heads of Europe; in 1871 he went to St. Petersburg to perform for the Czar of Russia, and was engaged to Princess Abemalik. She died and Shepard never married. In 1887 a wealthy San Diego rancher, William High, and other well-to-do townspeople donated the land and money to build the Villa Montezuma. Apparently, they built the house to entice Jesse Shepard to live in San Diego and bring culture to the small, flea-ridden, dusty frontier city. Shepard and his secretary, Lawrence Waldemar Tonner, remained in San Diego for only two years and, with the collapse of the land boom, were forced to sell the house at a loss so they could return part of the money to their benefactors. A public farewell concert was given by Shepard at the Unitarian Church. He ended the concert with his famous Grand Egyptian March in which he used the piano to simulate the sounds of marching, trumpets, battle clashes and cannon booms.

The Villa Montezuma remains today very much as it was described in an 1887 article in *The San Diego Union.* The original furnishings are gone, but the house is complete with period furnishings and has been open to the public as a museum and cultural center since 1970 under the auspices of The San Diego Historical Society. The exquisite polished woodwork and stained glass alone make this house a not-to-be-missed attraction in San Diego.

A dragon head seems to serve as a sentry at the southeast corner of the richly decorated mansion.

A bas-relief wooden plaque adorns the front of this historic home.

Decorative gable showing the 1887 construction date of the Villa.

THE VILLA MONTEZUMA

A portrait of Saint Cecilia in stained glass graces a stairwell.

Rich, carved redwood is found throughout the house.
Photo by Frank Borkat

1245 Island Avenue

A favorite subject for artists, this large Queen Anne Victorian is richly decorated with sunbursts, shingles, stained glass, and sawn decorative woodwork.

31

117 20th Street

A neighbor of the Villa Montezuma, this small Italianate-style house seems plain by comparison but has a charm of its own. Note the false front and decorative brackets. The house is a private residence.

515 20th Street

This handsome Italianate with its attractive arched windows and columned porch has been well cared for; it now serves as an apartment house.

670 20th Street

George Journeay was a housemover whose own home, built about 1895, stood at 20th and G. Still standing on the same corner, it is presently vacant and is to be restored. The semicircular balcony railing and fish-scale shingles are of particular interest. Journeay himself was a sort of local hero in San Diego. Whenever there was something difficult to be done, he was called upon. According to one story, in 1884 there was a torrential rainstorm and the telegraph lines northwest of San Diego were washed out. Journeay went out to prop up poles and restring wires. He got the line back into service, and when it was washed out a second time, he went out again and restrung wires. On his way back, unable to drive across the swollen San Dieguito River, he left his wagon at a nearby ranch, swam across, and hitched a ride home.

657 20th Street

This small Queen Anne cottage, built in 1890, is quaint and unique. The dormer windows are an outstanding feature. Versions of the sunburst may be seen on them and on the gables as well as at the upper corners of the large arched front window.

633 20th Street

This Queen Anne Victorian was condemned until recently and has now been completely restored. The pictures show the restoration in progress.

The sunburst was commonly used in Victorian architecture. Sunbursts are of many styles and shapes. Carol Olwell, in her book *A Gift to the Street*, offers this explanation: "Some say they represent the buoyant optimism of the Victorian era; others say it is the sun which never set on the once far-flung British Empire."

Restoration in progress

Restoration completed

37

2475 G Street

This eclectic design features interesting corner brackets and decorative spindle work along the front porch.

641 21st Street

This house has probably been altered somewhat since it was built in 1895, but the stickwork is of note. It is still used as a private residence.

Closeup of stickwork

631 21st Street

Small cottages were built and occupied by members of the working class, who could not afford the more extravagant architect-designed houses or the larger and more richly decorated Queen Anne style. Nonetheless, the builders used elements of Victorian architecture such as fish-scale shingles and sawn decorative scrollwork. Note the three different shingle styles adorning the gable of this tiny cottage. Built in the early 1890s, it is now a private residence.

1940 Market Street

Built in the late 1890s, this private residence has undoubtedly been altered, as many of the top balconies of Victorian houses have been enclosed to provide extra room. The spindles decorating the upper railing of the front porch are of particular interest.

Golden Hill

As the sun rolls down and is lost to sight,
Tinting the scene with its golden light,
The islands dim and the fading shore,
The ebbing tide through our harbor door,
The drooping sails of an anchoring fleet,
The shadowy city at our feet,
With the mountains proud peaks so lofty and still,
'Tis a picture worth seeing from Golden Hill.

Daniel Schuyler
Golden Era Magazine
March 1887

Golden Hill... The name was suggested by early residents Daniel Schuyler and Erastus Bartlett and given to the area* south of Balboa Park in 1887 (although the first land transaction took place in 1872). The setting sun often reflects off the hill in golden hue, and in the early days it was said to be possible to scoop up handfuls of gold-flecked dirt from the ground.

Whatever the reason for the name, Golden Hill had its "golden days" from about 1895-1925. Golden Hill Park was planted and watered by the residents, and boasted one of the city's first golf courses. In the early days, water was carried by hand to keep the trees and bushes green.

For 30 years Golden Hill was the fashionable place to live. Then the "gingerbread" houses with their towers, cupolas, imported stained glass windows and decorative scrollwork gradually began to chip and fade with age, their once proud facades showing signs of neglect. Prominent citizens of the city began to move to other areas, as public and private transportation became more available.

During the 1950s and '60s Golden Hill was considered a deteriorated area. Only the remaining run-down houses and some of the trees planted in Golden Hill Park by early residents were left to remind us of a more prosperous time.

But in recent years, a magical thing has begun to happen. The houses, one by one, are being restored, and their fresh paint jobs make a pleasant contrast to their once shabby appearance. Many young people have realized their worth as an investment and wish to preserve some of the past of Golden Hill. As a result, property values have risen once again and people are beginning to move back into the area. The formation of the Golden Hill Action Group has kindled a feeling of community pride and unity in Golden Hill.

The homes of several of the early prominent citizens of Golden Hill may be seen today. The interested tourist can enjoy many fine examples of well-preserved Victorian architecture, many within just a few blocks of one another.

---

* Bounded by A Street on the north, 94 on the south, 34th Street on the east and I-5 on the west.

42

845 20th Street

Built in 1887, this house bears a striking resemblance to the houses at 542 and 171 21st Street in Sherman Heights. The interior is currently being remodeled.

2404 Broadway

Historical Site #39

The Quartermass-Wilde House was first the home of Reuben Quartermass, a department store owner, and later of Louis Wilde, mayor of San Diego from 1917-1921. Wilde made many contributions to San Diego, including the fountain in Horton Plaza. The domed circular tower and corner entrance are among the dominant features of this late Victorian residence which has served as a music studio and religious center. It has now been adapted for office use.

THE QUARTERMASS-WILDE HOUSE , 1896

The tall stained glass windows are another striking feature of the Quartermass-Wilde House.

Many of the larger homes had their own carriage houses in the rear. This carriage house, behind the Quartermass-Wilde House, now serves as an apartment for the home's caretaker. The room in the original hayloft has a beautiful view of downtown and San Diego Bay.

838 25th Street

Built in 1890, this house was one of the early residences of Daniel Schuyler. Schuyler, who served as one of the city's first Park Commissioners, lived in Golden Hill for fifty years. The house is of neoclassical design, featuring a large first floor entry with Ionic columns and a gabled dormer. It is still a private residence and has been beautifully restored by its present owners.

850 22nd Street

A plain, almost homely little cottage, this charming redwood Victorian has sheltered San Diego's working class for many years. Its cozy appearance is well earned, as redwood is the wood most resistant to termites and it easily lasts 100 years. The cottage features stickwork ornamentation, common among the houses of the Victorian era.

1065 15th Street

A photography studio occupies
this charming Queen Anne tower
house which is dominated by the
octagonal tower.

3000 E Street THE FALK-KLAUBER HOUSE, 1888

Historical Site #122

In 1888, M.D. Falk built a house using redwood from his sawmill. It was purchased in 1892 by Abraham Klauber, a partner in a major wholesale grocery firm. When the Klaubers bought the house it was a long way out of town in an area known as Coyoteville (now 30th and E). The Klaubers lived there for many years and increased the size of the house by one-third.

When World War II broke out, the house was divided into fourteen apartments for defense workers. After the war it became successively a nursing home, boarding house, county jail, rehabilitation residence (the first halfway house in the United States), and finally an office building.

The present owner recently received permission to duplicate the original tower of the house and help restore the house to its original grandeur. The house also features carved redwood doors and keyhole window seats. The rock wall is original.

2441 E Street THE RYNEARSON HOUSE, 1898

Historical Site #121

Samuel Rynearson built his beautiful retirement home in 1898 at a cost of $5,000. Possibly designed by Irving Gill, it is eclectic in style and features a curving scrollwork frieze, a side portico, and a parapet. Today, Rynearson's home contains law offices.

1451 F Street

The frieze on the false front of this building is accented by the morning sun. During the 1890s the building was used as a laundry. The original laundry operator is unknown, but San Diego's Chinese residents were active in this business.

This "stairway to nowhere" is a sad and stark reminder of the elegant homes that must have stood in this now vacant, weed-covered and bottle-strewn lot located at 23rd and C Streets.

Cement contractors' stamps in sidewalks are a key to piecing together puzzles of the past. Unfortunately, some of them are not dated.

52

2124 Broadway

This house shows the true value of restoration. Obviously, had it been left to deteriorate further, it would have become an eyesore. Instead, it is being patiently restored by its present owners. The house is now a rental property and has been divided into apartments.

2456 Broadway

The A.H. Frost House at 2456 Broadway, of classical revival style, is an early creation of the famous architect Irving Gill. Built in 1897 for A.H. Frost, a bicycle manufacturer from Chicago who founded the Frost Hardwood Lumber Company in San Diego, the house appropriately was one of the first in San Diego to have fine hardwood floors. A leaded, beveled glass window enhances the beauty of the front door.

The house has served as a boarding house and convalescent home. Descendants of the original owner began restoring the house in 1976. It presently houses a number of shops.

2456 Broadway

1115 and 1117 19th Street

This house has probably been altered somewhat, but the fish-scale shingles and brackets are typical of the Victorian period and the house is picturesque with its white picket fence. It is a private residence and according to sewer records was probably divided into two apartments in 1948.

56

2148 Broadway THE HAYWARD-PATTERSON HOUSE

Historical Site #85

The Hayward-Patterson House at 22nd and Broadway was built in 1887 by Albert M. Hayward, captain of the yacht *San Diego*. The house was next owned by Francis Elliot Patterson, a professional photographer who owned a Fifth Avenue camera store and was largely responsible for the Title Insurance and Trust Company's photo collection. Patterson had been a first lieutenant in the army at the Mission of San Diego in 1851. His daughter Vida lived in the house until 1968 when she died at the age of 87. The house had fallen into disrepair until 1977 when restoration work was begun. This beautiful Italianate Victorian house is now one of several in Golden Hill that contain law offices.

2460 B Street

The white tower house at 2460 B Street was built in 1887 and was the home of Clark McKee, an attorney who started San Diego's first abstract and title company. His wife was on the women's board of the 1915 Panama-California Exposition. Their son Stewart flew kites from the tower of the house and rode ponies stabled by the Kellys on A Street. The McKee house features a peaked-roof tower with curved windows, and Doric columns on the porch. It is still used as a private residence.

THE NEW
NEIGHBORHOODS

Uptown 1880s

The Uptown area of San Diego (north of Date Street) consists of the districts and subdivisions of Banker's Hill, Cleveland Heights, Florence Heights, Middletown, and part of Horton's Addition.

The subdivision of Middletown was purchased and laid out in 1850 by ten men who hoped to make it the new location of the town. Nothing developed there for many years, but it eventually became one of the most valuable properties in the city. In 1886 lots were offered for sale for $125.00 each. By the end of 1887, electric, steam, and horse-drawn lines were bringing settlers to this and other outlying districts within the corporate limits of San Diego. Part of the Middletown area eventually became known as "Little Italy" because of the colony of Italian fishermen who settled there.

Horton's Addition was laid out in 1867 and the sections north of Date Street were mapped out in 1870. In 1868, 1400 acres of land adjacent to Horton's Addition were set aside for a park, which was later named Balboa Park.

In 1883 W.W. Bowers acquired an area bounded by 3rd, 4th, Fir, and Grape Streets. This was quite distant from Downtown at that time and many people thought him foolish when he built on his land the Florence Hotel, the most luxurious in all of San Diego. The view from the area was splendid in those days, stretching from the ocean to distant snowcapped peaks. The surrounding area became known as Florence Heights.

Cleveland Heights (bounded by Albatross Street, 1st Avenue, University Avenue, and Walnut Avenue) was named for Daniel Cleveland, a native of Poughkeepsie, New York, who arrived in San Diego on the steamship *Orizaba* in 1869. He was the attorney for the Texas and Pacific Railway Company and owned the subdivision known as Cleveland Heights. Cleveland was one of the founders of the San Diego Society of Natural History, San Diego's first hospital and summer school, a library, playgrounds, a bank, the Sons of the American Revolution Chapter, the Civic Federation to Combat Boss Rule, University Extension Society, San Diego Art Association, San Diego Tuberculosis Association, the YWCA, and the Pioneer Society. He led a move in 1872 to keep Balboa Park in the hands of the people. Author of a series of articles on San Diego history, Cleveland was one of the first San Diegans to engage in field botany.

Banker's Hill (west of Balboa Park and north of Florence Heights) before 1900 was an area where picnics and mushroom hunts were held. Quail and doves abounded in the canyons, and horse-drawn water carts were used to keep down the dust on the dirt roads. The streetcar line began serving the area in 1892, and after the turn of the century, with the coming of the automobile and paved streets, this area grew up and the population nearly doubled. Many bankers and other well-to-do families lived in the area in large well-kept homes resplendent with polished hardwood, stained glass windows, and adjacent carriage houses.

In recent years many of the beautiful old homes in the Uptown area have been turned into office buildings or businesses. The Britt-Scripps House, now a bed and breakfast house, is a prime example of imaginative preservation and reuse of historical structures.

406 Maple Street

THE BRITT-SCRIPPS HOUSE, 1887-88

Historical Site #52

The Britt-Scripps House was built for Eugene W. Britt, an attorney and president of the Los Angeles Bar Association. He formed a partnership with William Hunsaker in a prominent Southern California law firm. Britt served on the Supreme Court Commission and was one of the California delegates to the Republican National Convention in 1916. In 1896 the house was sold to E.W. Scripps, owner of the *San Diego Sun* and the *United Press*. After the Scripps family moved to their Miramar ranch, they retained ownership of the house for their use when they came to town.

The beautiful architectural details of the house make it a visual delight. The dramatic stained glass window on the west side of the house depicts morning, noon, and night. A variety of gables, dormers, and shingles give the house a typical Queen Anne design.

In 1979 the house was converted from a doctor's office and is now a popular San Diego bed and breakfast house.

THE BRITT-SCRIPPS HOUSE

1764 Columbia Street

This barn-style Dutch Victorian was built about 1892 by an unknown builder. The house is still a private residence.

1721 4th Avenue

This simple Italianate survives today as rental housing near downtown. Note the variations of the sunburst which appear below the square bay window.

66

2004 4th Avenue

The shingles are the outstanding feature, along with the decorated porch gable, of this residence built before the turn of the century. It now houses a graphic arts business.

2508 1st Avenue

Historical Site #38

The Timken House, built in 1888, is a late Victorian style, Queen Anne, with Georgian influence. The house was designed by the prominent architects Comstock & Trotsche.

The Timkens were prominent San Diego citizens involved in real estate and the fine arts. The Timken block downtown and the Timken Wing at the San Diego Museum of Art bear the family name. Mr. Timken, well-known inventor of the roller bearing, moved to San Diego for his retirement.

The house is resplendent in its detail; the shingles and spindles add a delicate look to this solid structure. It has been a private residence since 1965.

68

THE TIMKEN HOUSE, 1888

2408 1st Avenue

THE LONG-WATERMAN HOUSE, 1889

Historical Site #37

The first owners of this beautiful Queen Anne tower house had their occupancy cut short by deaths in their families. John Long, the first owner, headed the Coronado Fruit Package Company. He had the largest rotary veneer machine in the world and turned out the beautiful hardwoods used in the interior of the house. Mrs. Long drowned shortly after they moved in, and the house was next purchased in 1891 by Robert Whitney Waterman, seventeenth governor of California, for $17,000. Waterman was the owner of the San Diego, Cuyamaca, and Eastern Railroad and the Stonewall Mine. He lived there only a short time, however, before his death.

The house was sold in 1897 to Fred Root Hart and his wife Fanny, who lived there with their two daughters, May and Florence, and son Robert. Florence married Dr. Alfred Gilbert in 1908; a magnolia tree planted to commemorate the event still stands today. Alfred was the brother of the Gilbert sisters who lived together in the Sherman-Gilbert House downtown. Dr. and Mrs. Gilbert occupied the house after the Harts were deceased. In 1975 Florence Hart Gilbert died, having been preceded in death by her husband. Nearly eighty years of continuous occupancy by the Hart and Gilbert families were then ended.

For a time it appeared that the house would be demolished, as a buyer could not be found. Fortunately, John and Iris Parker purchased the house in 1977 and have restored it beautifully to its original grandeur. It is now headquarters for Parker Industries.

THE LONG-WATERMAN HOUSE

The unusual domed tower, the variety of shingle patterns, curved pane windows, long curved porch decorated with latticework, rounded bay windows, stained glass, and exquisitely adorned gables make the Long-Waterman House a visual feast of architectural details.

Porch, Long-Waterman House

73

THE LONG-WATERMAN HOUSE

Stained glass,
Long-Waterman House

74

South side, Long-Waterman House

75

1898 photograph of 2408 1st Avenue
Photograph courtesy of the San Diego
Historical Society — Title Insurance
and Trust Collection

76

2214-24 2nd Avenue

Probably the first design by Irving Gill and partner Joseph Falkenham, the Myles Moylan House was built in 1894 by Major Myles Moylan, a cavalry officer at the Battle of Little Big Horn when Custer was killed.

THE SHERMAN-DOIG HOUSE, 1887

Historical Site #104

John Sherman was the builder of this 1887 modified farmhouse stick-style structure. Sherman, a descendant of General William Tecumseh Sherman, built several houses in this area on land he bought from Alonzo Horton during the 1880s. The Sherman-Doig House was purchased in 1888 by Dr. John Rankin Doig, whose first San Diego office was at 5th and C Streets. In 1898, Dr. Doig moved to Kansas and became traveling surgeon for the Union Pacific Railroad.

The house changed hands many times until it was acquired in 1974 by SOHO and subsequently by its present owners. The "before" photograph shows how close the house was to being totally demolished. Now it is a showplace, visible from the freeway and beautifully lit at night.

Doig House before restoration
Photo courtesy of City of San Diego

1929 Front Street THE MUMFORD HOUSE, 1887

Historical Site #100

The angled bay windows of this stick-style 1887 Victorian capture a view of San Diego and the waterfront. The stick style features applied wooden ornamentation, and this is one of the types of Victorian architecture that is familiar in the tall, narrow row houses in San Francisco. The Mumford House is now the home of noted artist Robert Miles Parker, founder of SOHO. (See Sherman-Gilbert House, Heritage Park.)

2133 2nd Avenue THE BRODRICK-KENNEY HOUSE

Historical Site #136

This picturesque stick style with its latticework decoration and widow's walk was built during the land boom of 1886-1888 to help fill the need for rental housing for the well-to-do. Hotels in the city were overcrowded as businessman flocked to the newly created "boom city."

The house was well built of redwood and contains four fireplaces and one of the earlier electric elevators installed in a San Diego residence. It is presently an investment property.

3551 Front Street

This house (ca. 1895) is truly
unique. The fan decoration under
the bay window, the stained glass
window and sunbursts, the porch
railing, tower, and dormer
windows make this a true
showpiece of Victoriana.

230 Cedar Street

Plain cottage-style residences were occupied by the workers' families of early San Diego. The bay window and shingles are decorative touches.

1930 1st Avenue THE SHERMAN-JUDSON HOUSE

Historical Site #129

Built by John Sherman in 1887, this house was owned by County Assessor Frank Judson in 1895. Judson, who owned mine stock, raised horses and cattle, and sold real estate, purchased the house as an investment property. It was a middle-class house of its day and was one of two tract houses, the second of which was torn down in recent years. In 1947 it was converted to three apartments; today this well-restored Queen Anne Victorian houses law offices. It is one of three houses on which SOHO has taken a facade easement, which will insure its preservation for the future.

84

1907 Kettner Boulevard

This cottage in the Italian section of San Diego (ca. 1889) was originally built as a single-family residence and still is a private home. In 1935 the three Cornelia brothers, all fishermen, resided here.

2331 2nd Avenue

This asymmetrical Queen Anne, featuring several gables and an octagonal tower, is receiving a fanciful new paint job. It is currently a private residence.

4260 Campus Street

The Torrey House on Campus Street was occupied until 1905 by Eliza and Margaret Torrey who may have been the sisters of Dr. John Torrey for whom the Torrey pine was named. The inscription "Torreya" appears on the sidewalk in front of the house. This was the name given to the new evergreen tree discovered in the southwestern United States in 1838.

The unusual half-arched entrance is an outstanding feature of this large Queen Anne Victorian. The house was built in Normal Heights when developers had high hopes for this area. The Torrey House presently contains apartments.

4366 Maryland Street

In 1914, the house at 4366 Maryland was purchased by Delia Augusta Curtis. She lived there until her death in 1915. The property then passed to her nieces Delia and Rena and was sold in 1916 to Susan G. Johnson, a school teacher, who lived there for many years. Delia Augusta (Gussie) Curtis and her sister Sarah Henrietta (Etta) began a private kindergarten in San Diego in 1877. It is believed to have been the first kindergarten in San Diego. They operated the school for 20 years and were the first teachers of Miss Mary Marston. Today the house is in an excellent state of preservation and is still a private residence.

208 West Laurel Street

This boarding house was recently demolished (May 1981).
The unusual wooden molding was intricately detailed.

136 Juniper Street

THE TORRANCE HOUSE, 1887

Historical Site #94

The Torrance House, once owned by A.E. Horton, is being beautifully restored by its present owners. Built in 1887, it was the home of Elisha Swift Torrance, a highly respected lawyer in early San Diego who was elected three times to the Superior Court bench. The stained glass windows are original, and the decorative frieze and open arched gable are charming accents.

136 Juniper Street

321 West Walnut Avenue

Built in 1891 for Letitia Lovett, this house was moved in 1911 to its present location from 4th and Walnut on logs drawn by horses.

Commander Bert McVey then moved in, having purchased the house from H.H. Timken (son of Henry) who wanted to build a more modern home at 4th and Walnut. In the 1920s, stucco was applied over the wood lap siding, but the house still retains much of its earlier charm.

110 Juniper Street

Adaptive reuse at its best is shown in this professional office building. In the 1880s it was the home of W.J. Hunsaker, District Attorney for San Diego County, and Mayor in 1887. The house was restored in 1979.

836 East Washington Street

Historical Site #134

Construction of St. Joseph's Sanitarium, founded by the Sisters of Mercy, began in 1891. The house at 836 East Washington Street is the only remaining building of the sanitarium. The house was moved here in 1920 from its earlier site near 8th and University. It is a good example of a late 19th century cottage and presently houses professional offices.

One of the earliest San Diego cement contractors' stamps.

95

1767 2nd Avenue THE WATTS HOUSE, ca. 1896

Historical Site #57

This small but richly decorated cottage was altered when the front porch to the right of the bay window was closed in. The dentil course frieze and scrolled wood brackets give a rich texture. The house was moved from 7th and C Streets sometime before 1906.

3408 6th Avenue

A beautifully detailed Queen Anne Victorian features decorative shingles and brackets and a columned portico.

3620 Front Street

This charming Victorian home was built for Mrs. Frank Grandier, a native of Switzerland who was active in county government and founder in 1907 of *The Daily Transcript*. It is built of redwood with square nails. From 1910 to 1939 it was the residence of Richard Benbough, brother of an early San Diego mayor (1930). His wife Louise was a nurse who helped care for the victims of the explosion of the gunboat U.S.S. *Bennington* in 1905. The house, presently a private residence, features a sunburst gable that is almost identical to the ones at 1610 and 1632 Union Street.

Gable, 3620 Front Street

3131 5th Avenue

A squared farmhouse-style Victorian

2425 1st Avenue

This very unusual style is charming with its wavy shingles and sunburst fans.

3544 Front Street

An unusual double-porched cottage

103

Logan Heights

The glory of Logan Heights is long faded. Yet here are to be found some treasures of Victoriana well worth saving. Bounded roughly by Imperial Avenue on the north, I-5 on the south and 47th Street on the east, Logan Heights extends southward to about where National City begins.

Developed during the 1880s and '90s, Logan Heights derived its name from Logan Avenue, one of a series of streets in the neighborhood named for military and political figures — this one honoring Army Major General John A. Logan.

Early Logan Heights landowners were attracted by the promise of a transcontinental railroad terminal in the area. Because of the 1873 stock market crash, the dream of a transcontinental railroad was not realized until 1885, and then the depot was built at the foot of D (Broadway) in San Diego. Still people came to Logan Heights for the fertile soil, ocean view, level ground and accessibility to the business district of downtown San Diego. They built Victorian-style homes on streets that were laid out in a northwesterly to southeasterly direction. This street plan allowed for the sun to shine into every room of every house at some time during the day.

During the 1890s commercial transportation and industry began to spread through Logan Heights. One of San Diego's early streetcar lines plied the streets here, and a railroad trunk line connected the area with Downtown, making the area ideal for the location of industrial plants. Industry boomed, and slowly its attraction as a residential community declined.

During the 1930s and '40s the original residents of Logan Heights were moving to other more desirable spots away from industry in the city, leaving behind a legacy of Victorian architecture.

The residential population decreased rapidly as industry grew in the 1940s and '50s. The 1970s saw a leveling off and then a decline in both industrial and residential growth. Logan Heights was a decaying section of the city.

The building of Chicano Park in 1971 has helped to foster a sense of community awareness sadly lacking in Logan Heights in recent years. While Logan Heights does not presently seem to be progressing as quickly as Golden Hill, some improvements are noticeable, and it can be reasonably hoped that many examples of Victorian architecture will be preserved.

2042 Kearny Avenue THE GORHAM HOUSE

Historical Site #138

The Gorham House was built in 1894 by Cornelius Gorham, a building contractor. It features one of the few examples of iron roof cresting in San Diego. The shingles and decorative brackets add to the interest of this well-kept home.

2146 Newton Avenue

This Italianate private residence (ca. 1885) features diagonal wood accents on the bay windows. The house has been beautifully maintained.

106

2981 Boston Avenue

A single-story Italianate (ca. 1880) features sawtooth wooden detailing. It was probably moved from another site.

1851 Irving Avenue

This Italianate (ca. 1885) has a
squared Queen Anne tower and
arched windows. The house was
moved to its present site and a
room added over the side porch.

2241 Irving Avenue

A richly decorated cottage with sawn decorative scrollwork and spindle detailing.

2054 Kearny Avenue

This Italianate is in need of repair but is charming even so with its decorative brackets, porch posts and squared bay windows.

2054 Julian Avenue

Note the juxtaposition of shingles on the gable of this Queen Anne cottage (ca. 1895) and the interesting finial on the peak of the gable. In 1926 this modest cottage was occupied by a U.S. Grant Hotel laundry employee.

111

729 S. 32nd Street

This Queen Anne tower house (ca. 1895) is decorated with fishscale shingles, sunburst brackets and latticework detailing on the porch.

112

3139 Franklin Avenue

Historical Site #78

This house was built in 1885 at the corner of 7th and D Streets by Albert M. Hayward. It was moved to its present site in 1902. It is the only house in San Diego with a ship's cabin cupola. Other interesting features are the Ionic columns at the entryway and the park-like grounds with statues, fountains and greenery.

2060 Kearny Avenue

A Queen Anne with a decorative bargeboard on each gable and an unusual second-story porch, ca. 1890. This house appears not to have been altered.

2084 Kearny Avenue

The value of housing rehabilitation is shown by the restoration of this Queen Anne Victorian. The house is acquiring a new foundation.

2660 National Avenue

An excellent example of the Italianate style. No major alterations appear to have been made. The double front door and sawn decorations adorning the front porch help to make this house unique.

The Beach Communities

The communities of Pacific Beach, Point Loma, and La Jolla were all sparsely settled during the latter part of the 19th century. Because of a collapse in San Diego's land boom and because some of the few Victorian houses were moved or demolished, very few Victorian houses are to be found in these areas today.

La Jolla and Pacific Beach were first subdivided and lots offered for sale in 1887. By 1888 the San Diego, Old Town and Pacific Beach Railroad took passengers to the junction where it turned off to Pacific Beach, and from there the trip to La Jolla was made by horse and wagon. Finally in 1894 the railroad was extended to La Jolla.

By 1889 there were 100 permanent residents in Pacific Beach. The tract had been laid out with wide avenues and parks. Pacific Beach boasted a race track (Wyatt Earp raced his horse there), a post office and weekly newspaper, wide beaches, a healthful climate, and fishing and duck hunting. The San Diego College of Letters, located at Garnet and Lamont, offered the only higher education available in San Diego.

The end of the land boom left Pacific Beach partially deserted. Many of the people remaining began growing lemons, and Pacific Beach became a lemon shipping center. Eventually the orchards were destroyed as subdivisions developed in the area.

During the early days in La Jolla fresh water was scarce and had to be hauled in from Rose Canyon in whiskey barrels.

Twice a week a wagon load of food and supplies came in from Pacific Beach. These factors probably partially accounted for the slow population growth.

By 1907, La Jolla had a year-round population of approximately 500 — largely wealthy retired people, authors and artists who enjoyed their isolation from other communities. A small thriving tourist industry catered to an elite clientele who traveled here in search of peace and harmony beside the sea, but La Jolla remained sparsely populated until after World War I.

The settlement of Point Loma was begun in the 1850s by Louis Rose, the first Jewish resident of San Diego. He planned to make Point Loma a townsite for the employees of his manufacturing enterprises. Plans were made for Point Loma to be the terminus of the San Diego and Gila, Southern Pacific and Atlantic Railroad, but it never got beyond the surveying stage. After the failure to secure a railroad terminus, development did not begin in earnest until the late 1880s, and by 1892 there were still few residents on Point Loma. Louis Rose's dream of making Roseville — rather than San Diego — the major city had not materialized, and Roseville remained a military base and residential community.

The few examples of Victorian architecture in the beach communities are prized for their uniqueness and have been well cared for. Most of them are private residences today.

1576 Law Street

This charming house was built in 1892 by Victor Hinkle, a lemon grower who moved to San Diego from Kansas and copied the Midwest architectural syle. The house first stood on Chalcedony Street and was surrounded by a 10-acre lemon grove. The land was gradually sold, and in the 1930s the house was moved to its present location. It features an iron cresting and flower-pattern stained glass windows.

121

1704 Grand Avenue

A turn-of-the-century
farmhouse in Pacific Beach.

122

1018 Rosecrans Street THE JENNINGS HOUSE

Historical Site #55
Historical Landmark #85

The Colonial-style Jennings House, last of the Roseville residences, has undergone many alterations and restorations. Built in 1888, today it houses legal offices.

The Jennings brothers are credited with being among the most influential forces in the development of Point Loma. After the founding of Roseville by Louis Rose, the Jennings brothers devoted 20 years to developing this section of San Diego. They built a factory, the nail mill, and a steamboat, the *Roseville*. The *Roseville* transported potential land buyers from San Diego to Roseville. Today the Jennings House is all that remains of their efforts.

3838 Dixon Place

This tantalizing view is as close as one can get to the Dixon House on Point Loma. The house was built about 1895 by Albert Dixon for his widowed sister-in-law, from lumber that had made up a nail factory in Roseville, an early Point Loma subdivision. An olive grove once grew on nine acres of surrounding land but the property has been subdivided several times. The house today is a private residence and is still in the Dixon family.

7212 La Jolla Blvd. GALUSHA B. GROW COTTAGE

Historical Site #133

The Galusha B. Grow Cottage, built in 1895, is vernacular Victorian, a style popular at the turn of the century. Galusha Grow was active in early San Diego banking and was a fire commissioner. This cottage was probably his vacation home. The entrance, set at a 45-degree angle, is an outstanding feature. The cottage was moved from Ivanhoe Street in 1980 to Heritage Place-La Jolla (Historical Site 128) and is now a private residence. Heritage Place has been established as a place where a few early La Jolla cottages, threatened with demolition, can be moved and restored.

7590 Draper Avenue

Miss Florence Sawyer moved to La Jolla in 1895 and bought the "Red Rest" cottage. In 1898 she donated the land and erected a building for a Reading Room at the corner of Girard and Wall Streets. She presented the Reading Room to the village along with $1,000 worth of books. The building was used for club meetings and social events as well as for a library. When the new library was built the Reading Room was moved to Draper Avenue where it stands today as a private residence. The building today looks very much as it did in 1898.

7851 Drury Lane

Olivia McGilvery Mudgett was the sister of Mrs. Anson P. Mills, a prominent early citizen of La Jolla. "Livy" was active in La Jolla social life and was the second president of the La Jolla Woman's Club. Her house, "Villa Waldo," was built in 1894 on Girard Avenue (then Grand) and later was moved to the back of the same lot. It then faced on Drury Lane and was known as the Jenny Wren apartments. The house has recently been remodeled.

2203 Denver St. THE STOUGH-BECKETT HOUSE

ca. 1888   Historical Site #146

The Stough-Beckett House, built during the San Diego land boom, was planned to be a part of the subdivision of Morena where it was hoped a new townsite would take root. The Morena Company, with O.J. Stough as its principal owner, built the house for speculation or to provide lodging for its carpenters. The end of the land boom, however, saw the demise of the townsite, and only sixteen houses had been constructed at its height.

In 1920 James Beckett bought this house; it remained in his family until 1977. Beckett operated a small lunchroom in downtown San Diego. Today there are only three houses of the land boom era standing in Morena, and the Stough-Beckett House is being carefully restored by its present owners. Some of the wooden detailing has been temporarily removed and a new paint job is in progress. The house is a simple style (probably a pattern house) and is one of the earliest examples of tract housing in San Diego.

128

ONE HUNDRED
YEARS LATER

Heritage Park 1971

Victorian houses line a cobblestone walk, picturesque with lamp posts and benches in San Diego's seven-acre Heritage Park (located near Old Town). Small shops, a travel agency, a restaurant and offices occupy the houses, all of which were moved here in an effort to save them from destruction.

In 1969 the concept of a park where endangered Victorian structures could be preserved was born in the early meetings of a group of San Diego nostalgia buffs, who called themselves Save Our Heritage Organisation (SOHO); their plans were implemented by the Board of Supervisors.

The park's first acquisition, the Sherman-Gilbert House, was saved from demolition through the efforts of a young San Diego artist, Robert Miles Parker, the founder of SOHO. With the cooperation of San Diego County, the group grew rapidly. It raised enough money to halt the wrecking crew and move the house to county property at a site near the present Heritage Park. After it was moved to the park in 1971 the house stood

on blocks for three years while the County decided what to do with it. It was finally renovated as an office for the County Parks and Recreation Department.

In 1976, three additional houses were moved to the park, and questions arose as to who would be permitted to occupy the space. It was finally decided, in order to preclude the possibility of a Disneyland atmosphere in the park, to lease small spaces to individuals rather than leasing the entire park to a single individual or corporation.

Since Heritage Park is a public park, supported by tax dollars, it must appeal to a broad cross-section of the population, and not just historians. It must generate income to offset costs. The individual lessees in the park are responsible for restoring the interiors of the houses, while county and federal matching funds are used to restore the exteriors. County and donated money (some from SOHO) helped to move the houses, and county funds are used for landscaping, improvements, and parking.

Another problem arose when San Diego County proposed the building of replica structures in order to finish the park in time for the Bicentennial celebration in 1976. Park proponents objected strenuously to the use of replicas, and a decision was eventually reached that all buildings in the park must be actual structures of the Victorian era, 1880-1900, and must be historically or architecturally significant.

Since then the Senlis Cottage, Temple Beth Israel, the McConaughy House, and a carriage house have been relocated in Heritage Park. Future development will probably depend upon the amount of money available, but already the people of San Diego have a magnificent park in which to spend a pleasant day shopping and browsing amidst relics of San Diego's colorful past.

Sherman-Gilbert House — HERITAGE PARK

Historical Site #8

Built in 1887, the Sherman-Gilbert House was saved from demolition in 1971 by the formation of Save Our Heritage Organisation, when its original location at 139 Fir Street was to become the site of a parking lot for Centre City Hospital. This unusual house has one of the few circular windows in a San Diego Victorian home. The house is heavily embellished with latticework, stickwork, and scrollwork, and features a widow's walk.

The architects of this 20-room, $20,000 house were Comstock and Trotsche, a distinguished firm in early San Diego. The builder, John Sherman, lived in the house for a short time. The house was sold to the Gilberts in 1897, and it remained in the Gilbert family until 1965. After their parents died, Bess and Gertrude Gilbert lived in the house. They were active in the arts and entertained many famous people in the house, including the Trapp Family Singers, Marian Anderson, Madame Ernestine Schumann-Heink, and Yehudi Menuhin. After Gertrude died in 1947, Bess lived there alone until her death in 1965.

A few small alterations were made to the house, including removal of the tower in 1940 to conform to requirements of buildings in the flight pattern of Lindbergh Field. The tower was later restored. The Sherman-Gilbert House was the first one to be moved to Heritage Park and presently houses a shop and an art gallery.

132

Christian House — HERITAGE PARK

The home of Harfield Timberlake Christian, this beautiful Queen Anne tower house was built in 1889. The original location was 1940 Third Avenue. Christian was very active in San Diego civic affairs. He served as alderman, city clerk, city assessor, Deputy U.S. Marshal, U.S. Commissioner, and was on the Board of Freeholders which formed the city charter. Christian was president of San Diego Title and Insurance Company. The house, which has not been substantially altered, was moved to Heritage Park in 1975 and is now a restaurant, recreating a Victorian atmosphere.

133

Bushyhead House — HERITAGE PARK

Built in 1887 for use as a rental house, the Bushyhead House was formerly located at 232 Cedar Street. This stick-style Victorian, a rental for 50 years, had been badly vandalized when it was acquired by SOHO in 1978.

Edward Wilkerson Bushyhead, the builder, was descended from a Cherokee Indian mother whose son was given the name "Bushyhead" because of his full head of hair and his beard. Thereafter, it remained the family's surname. Bushyhead was an early San Diego sheriff and one of the first owners of *The San Diego Union*. He came to California for the gold rush and met Jeff Gatewood, a San Diego publisher. The two established *The San Diego Union* from which Bushyhead resigned in 1873. Today, the Bushyhead House is occupied by a number of shops.

134

The Burton House — HERITAGE PARK

Classic Revival is the style of the Burton House, built in 1893 and formerly located at 1970 Third Avenue. This style was "late Victorian," moving away from the heavier gingerbread ornamentation of the 1880s. It was the home of Dr. Henry Guild Burton, an army ophthalmologist who settled in San Diego after serving in the army in the San Diego barracks.

The house was owned by only four families in the 82 years it was a private residence and was mostly owner-occupied. Between 1905 and 1943 the house was renovated several times. The last private owner, a physician, donated the house to the Diabetes Association for use as its offices. A travel agency and specialty shops now occupy the Burton House.

Senlis Cottage — HERITAGE PARK

The Senlis Cottage was a workingman's cottage with no gas, electricity, water, or sewer hookups. Originally located at 1536 2nd Avenue, it was first the home of Eugene Senlis, an employee of Kate Sessions. In later years it was home at various times to a store clerk, a woman barber, and a carpenter. Will Hippen, honorary Consul General to Japan, donated the house to Save Our Heritage Organisation in 1978, and it now serves as their headquarters.

Temple Beth Israel — HERITAGE PARK

The Temple Beth Israel is the oldest or second oldest such structure in the West. It is certainly the oldest synagogue in Southern California. Victorian eclectic in style and built by an unknown builder, the temple was used for the first time on Rosh Hashanah eve, September 25, 1889.

In about 1926 the congregation outgrew and sold the temple, but bought it back and donated it to the county in 1978 when it was moved to Heritage Park from 1502 2nd Avenue. The building, which had had no exterior alterations, is currently being refurbished for use as a community meeting hall.

McConaughy House — HERITAGE PARK

The McConaughy House was built in 1887 for John McConaughy who started a passenger and freight line between San Diego and Julian. He later worked with his son James in real estate. A later owner, Mrs. Keating, donated the house for temporary use as a hospital when one was needed in 1889. In 1890 the hospital was closed for repairs and in 1895 it was known as the Good Samaritan Home. The house was later turned back to Mrs. Keating and after 1936 was used as a multiple dwelling.

The McConaughy House originally stood at 1569 Union Street as it did when this photograph was taken. It was moved to Heritage Park in 1981. Most recently used as attorneys' offices, this Italianate Victorian appears not to have been altered since the hospital remodeling. After its relocation and refurbishing the McConaughy House will once again be occupied by its law tenants.

Heritage Park from Senlis Cottage

139

Epilogue

Relics from the past — yesterday's commonplace objects — can be today's treasures, living links to times gone by. Our souvenirs are reminders that the past is not dead at all, and that what we are now is somehow a culmination of all who have gone before. To close the door upon our past would be sad indeed, for to preserve from our past is to provide for our future.

Precious souvenirs are those romantic, frivolous, wonderful Victorian houses where our grandmothers may have lived. Yet the question of "economic feasibility" is one of the harsh realities of the present. In many cases, moving a house to a spot where it can serve as a tourist attraction is an answer.

While the answers are being found for preservation of San Diego Victoriana, it is hoped that this book will be used, not only as a picture book, but as a guide book for the interested "souvenir hunter." Armed with this book and a map, the intrepid adventurer may discover houses, streets and entire neighborhoods he or she has never seen before, and experience a new appreciation of San Diego's architectural heritage.

Glossary of Terms

Eastlake

Most "Eastlake" style houses could be classified as Stick or Queen Anne style except for the distinguishing Eastlake features which include applied ornamentation (often floral) which was largely a product of the chisel, gouge, and lathe; curved brackets; posts that resemble table legs; rows of spindles along porches or verandahs; knobs of various forms; and decorative motifs consisting of circular perforations.

Gothic Revival

An architectural style characterized by high pitched roofs, pointed arches, high gables with bargeboards, and occasional medieval features.

Historic American Buildings Survey

Inclusion in this survey means that scale drawings of the house have been made and are housed in HABS headquarters. HABS is under the authority of the U.S. Department of the Interior, National Parks Service, Washington, D.C., and is a joint project with the American Institute of Architects.

Historical Landmark

A state designation given by the California State Historical Resources Commission. Architectural landmarks are considered significant if they are prototypes or if they are outstanding examples of a period, style, architectural movement or method of construction, or if they are the most notable works or the best surviving work in a given region of a pioneer architect, designer, or a master builder. The applicant for Historical Landmark registration must give assurance to the best of his or her ability that the site will be perpetuated as a historical landmark. Any action that destroys the significance that was the basis for the landmark's designation may be grounds for registration withdrawal.

Historical Site

A local designation given by the San Diego Historical Site Board. A historical site is defined as any site (including significant trees or other plant life located thereon), building, structure, or mark having historical significance because of its association with such things as noted past events, historical persons, or distinguishing architectural characteristics. A permit for the demolition, substantial alteration, or removal of a historical site may not be issued without the matter being referred to the Historical Site Board, except when the City Manager determines that such demolition, alteration, or removal is necessary for the public health, safety, or welfare. Further, any trees, plants, or other major landscaping may not be removed from the property designated as a historical site without prior approval of the City Manager.

Italianate

An architectural style characterized by rounded or arched window heads, controlled vertical forms and details, regularly spaced ornamental brackets under the eaves, wood or cast iron railings at porch or roof line, flat or low pitched roofs, and elaborate cornices. This style is sometimes rather severely cube-shaped in general outline and occasionally includes angled bay windows and small porticoes with classic columns.

National Register of Historic Places

A national historic landmark register administered by the Keeper of the Register, U.S. Department of the Interior, Washington, D.C. The Register is the nation's official list of cultural resources worthy of preservation. Designation does not affect title to the property; however, in order to destroy or substantially alter a property included in the Register, an environmental impact report may be necessary. Projects that threaten a National Register landmark must first undergo review by citizens and units such as the Office of Historic Preservation. National Register properties are eligible for grants-in-aid, federally guaranteed loans, property tax relief, and federal tax incentives for rehabilitating income-producing properties.

Pattern Book Houses

Houses which were built according to plans and specifications found in a book or magazine. They were often the smaller, less ornate houses.

Queen Anne

An architectural style that incorporates many varied elements. Some of these are varied roof lines; cut-out corners; contrasting colors; irregular elevations; an assortment of surfaces; and a variety of chimneys, towers, bay windows, verandahs, bargeboards, arches, balconied porches, leaded glass windows, and shingles.

Stick

An architectural style characterized by tall proportions, steep roofs, wide eaves supported by large brackets, extensive verandahs, and decorative stickwork (application of boards to the exterior of a house in a manner that suggests the unseen structural frame).

143

BIBLIOGRAPHY

The author's original interest and chief concern in compiling this book has been the photographing of the lovely Victorian homes of San Diego, recording them on film before too many more vanish forever. She has spent almost three years poring over documents and research files in search of historical background material on these homes; *Timeless Treasures* does not, however, pretend to be the definitive historical authority on the Victorians.

The following bibliography lists the major sources of information the author used in preparation of this book.

Published Sources

Baer, Morley; Pomada, Elizabeth; and Larsen, Michael. *Painted Ladies.* New York: E. P. Dutton, 1978.

Banaszewski, John. "Heritage Park, an Identity Crisis." *San Diego Daily Transcript,* November 19, 1979.

Bigger, Richard; Musolf, Lyndon R.; Kitchen, James D.; and Quinn, Carolyn. *Metropolitan Coast: San Diego and Orange Counties, California.* Los Angeles: Bureau of Governmental Research, UCLA, 1958.

Black, Samuel F. *History of San Diego County, California.* Chicago: The S.J. Clarke Publishing Company, 1913.

Blumenson, John J.G. *Identifying American Architecture: A Pictorial Guide to Styles and Terms, 1600-1945.* Nashville: American Association for State and Local History, 1977.

Branin, Jeannette. "Long Lost Manuscript Tells Romantic Story." *The San Diego Union,* August 12, 1973.

"Renaissance Comes to Golden Hill After Period of Deterioration." *The San Diego Union,* April 1, 1973.

Craft, Eileen. "They Don't Build Them Like This Anymore." *San Diego Sentinel,* November 15, 1978.

Crane, Clare. "Matthew Sherman: Pioneer San Diegan." *The Journal of San Diego History* 18 (1972): 22-27.

"Area History." *San Diego Model Cities Neighborhood Business Directory,* 1971-72, 4-5.

D'Alfonso, Virginia, Ed. *Survivors.* Santa Barbara: The Santa Barbara Historical Society, 1979.

"Early Empire Builders Planned Great Industrial City and Railroad Terminus on Point Loma." *Ocean Beach News,* January 1, 1937.

Engstrand, Iris W. *San Diego: California's Cornerstone.* Tulsa: Continental Heritage Press Inc., 1980.

Gebhard, David, and Winter, Robert. *A Guide to Architecture in Los Angeles and Southern California.* Santa Barbara and Salt Lake City: Peregrine Smith, Inc., 1977.

Gillon, Edmund V., Jr., and Lancaster, Clay. *Victorian Houses: A Treasury of Lesser-Known Examples.* New York: Dover Publications, Inc., 1973.

Heritage Landmarks: Right Next Door. California Heritage Bank.

Heritage Park: Created for the Preservation of San Diego's Victorian Era. A San Diego County Regional Park booklet.

Johnson, Nancy. "Victorian Home One of Four Stars: Banker's Hill Vaults Into Tour Spotlight." *San Diego Evening Tribune,* June 1, 1972.

La Jolla: The Jewel City. San Diego: Union Title Insurance and Trust Company, 1951.

Lawrence, Herb. "Supervisors Reject Heritage Park Lease." *The San Diego Tribune,* June 29, 1977.

"Local Brevities." *The San Diego Union,* February 23, 1884; March 11, 1884; March 18, 1884; April 12, 1884.

Locker, Zelma Bays. "Whatever Happened to Izard Street? Pacific Beach and Its Street Names." *The Journal of San Diego History* 22 (1976): 20-29.

"Logan Heights Holds Top Spot in San Diego History." *The San Diego Union*, May 30, 1937.

"Lure of La Jolla as Year Around Resort Traced to Early Trips of Indians." *The San Diego Sun*, May 29, 1938.

Marston, Mary Gilman. *George White Marston: A Family Chronicle.* Los Angeles: The Ward Ritchie Press, 1956.

McMullen, Jerry. "Roughing it in La Jolla." *The San Diego Union*, June 28, 1963.

MacPhail, Elizabeth C. *The Story of New San Diego and of its Founder Alonzo E. Horton.* San Diego: San Diego Historical Society, 1979.

Mills, John S. *San Diego, California.* San Diego: Board of Supervisors and the Chamber of Commerce of San Diego County, California, 1908.

Mimms, Ken. "Costs Slow Heritage Park Lease." *The San Diego Union*, September 2, 1978.

Montes, Gregory W. "San Diego's City Park, 1868-1902: An Early Debate on Environment and Profit." *The Journal of San Diego History* 23 (1977): 40-45.

Olwell, Carol and Waldhorn, Judith Lynch. *A Gift to the Street.* San Francisco: Antelope Island Press, 1976.

Pourade, Richard F. *The Glory Years.* San Diego: The Union-Tribune Publishing Company, 1964.

Randolph, Howard S.F. *La Jolla Year by Year.* La Jolla: The Library Association of La Jolla, 1955.

San Diego Chapter of the American Institute of Architects. *AIA Guide to San Diego.* San Diego, 1977.

San Diego City Directories, 1887-1900.

The San Diego Federal Writer's Project, Works Progress Administration, State of California. *San Diego, A California City.* San Diego: San Diego Historical Society, 1937.

Schaelchlin, Patricia. "Morena: A Small Cottage Gets New Life in an Early San Diego Suburb." *San Diego Home/Garden,* February 1981, 26-28.

"Rynearson Mansion: It Symbolizes Past Glories on Golden Hill." *San Diego Home/Garden.* July 1980, 44-48.

"The Lovett House on Banker's Hill: It's in Queen Anne, A Victorian Style That Saved Energy." *San Diego Home/Garden,* June 1980, 52-56.

Schwartz, Henry. "History of Historic Temple." *San Diego Jewish Press Heritage,* December 1, 1978.

Scott, Ed. *San Diego County Soldiers-Pioneers 1846-1866.* National City: Crest Printing Company, 1976.

Showley, Roger. "Old Town Park Plans Told." *The San Diego Union,* August 5, 1977.

Smythe, William E. *History of San Diego 1542-1908.* San Diego: The History Company, 1908.

Stern, Norton B., and Kramer, William M. "The Rose of San Diego." *The Journal of San Diego History* 19 (1973): 27-39.

Stevens, Gus. "Heritage Park Plan Hums Anew." *The San Diego Tribune,* August 7, 1976.

"Victorian Era House Brought Back to Grace." *The San Diego Tribune,* March 31, 1977.

Stevenson, Kenneth. *The History of San Diego Real Estate.* San Diego: 1938.

Stone, Joe. "Point Loma Home, Tower, Trees, A Showcase." *The San Diego Union,* May 7, 1972.

Tourists Guide to San Diego. San Diego: Frank H. Mandeville, Publisher, 1888.

Wagner, Harr, ed. "The Building of San Diego." *The Golden Era* 36 (1887): 249-253.

"Development of the San Diego Bay Region: Pacific Beach." *The Golden Era* 36 (1887): 762-763.

Whiffen, Marcus. *American Architecture Since 1780: A Guide to the Styles.* Cambridge and London: The MIT Press, 1969.

Unpublished Sources

"Banker's Hill." San Diego Historical Society Third Annual Historical Homes Tour booklet.

Barley, Patrick, and Pearlman, Michael. "Barrio Logan and Western Southeast San Diego Historical Survey." City of San Diego Historical Site Board, June 1980.

Benbough, Richard. "Residence of Merit in Architectural Heritage." Unpublished Manuscript, San Diego Historical Society Library and Manuscripts Collection.

Biographical Files, San Diego Historical Society Library and Manuscripts Collection.
Cleveland, Daniel
Torrance, Judge E.S.
Torrey, Mrs. Herbert Gray
Torrey, Dr. John

Box Files, San Diego Historical Society Library and Manuscripts Collection.
Houses, Buildings, Streets, etc.
Houses, Housing, Streets, Street Names
Real Estate
San Diego Information Prior to 1910 (Publicity)

Crane, Clare. "A Partial List of Victorian Buildings in San Diego." Unpublished notes, San Diego Historical Society Library and Manuscripts Collection.

"Logan Heights: An Historical Survey Compiled and Presented by Clare Crane." September 1971. San Diego Historical Society Library and Manuscripts Collection.

"Golden Days in Golden Hills." Pamphlet for the Second Annual Historic Homes Tour, 1967.

Greater Golden Hill District Proposal. September 1978.

Harris, LeRoy E. "The Other Side of the Freeway." Dissertation for the degree of Doctor of Arts, Carnegie-Mellon University, 1974.

Hensley, Herbert C. *The Memoirs of Herbert C. Hensley, History of San Diego City, County, and Region.* Typescript bound in five vols. San Diego Historical Society Library and Manuscripts Collection.

Historical Site Board Registers and Reports.

Historic Resources Inventory for Middletown Area, San Diego, California. University of San Diego, April 1980.

MacPhail, Elizabeth Curtis. The Curtis Family 1877-1969. Curtis Family Box File, San Diego Historical Society Library and Manuscripts Collection.

Sanborn Fire Map 1887. California Room, San Diego Public Library.

The San Diego Union Newspaper Files. California Room, San Diego Public Library.

Save Our Heritage Organisation, vertical files.

SOHO "Reflections."
"Golden Hills: Withering Heights." November 1975.
"Thumbnail Tour: The 'Torrey' House of Normal Heights." Undated.
"Gingerbread Monument Threatened: Time Running Out On Long-Waterman-Gilbert House." February 1977.

SOHO. Uptown-Middletown Tour booklet, 1981.

Swain, L. "The New Guide, Subject: Golden Hill." Unpublished manuscript, San Diego Historical Society Library and Manuscripts Collection.

Tabler, Joseph. "A General Historical Researching of the Barrio Logan." Unpublished manuscript, San Diego Historical Society Library and Manuscripts Collection.

Uptown Community Plan. Uptown Planners and the City of San Diego, May 1975.

Water and Utilities Department, water and sewer records. City of San Diego.